Parenting in the Age of Columbine

Parenting in the Age of Columbine

Poems by

Elizabeth S. Wolf

© 2025 Elizabeth S. Wolf. All rights reserved.
This material may not be reproduced in any form, published,
reprinted, recorded, performed, broadcast,
rewritten or redistributed without
the explicit permission of Elizabeth S. Wolf.
All such actions are strictly prohibited by law.

Cover design by Shay Culligan
Cover image by Annie Spratt on Unsplash
Author photo by Samantha Graves (2025)

ISBN: 978-1-63980-851-9
Library of Congress Control Number: 2025950962

Kelsay Books
502 South 1040 East, A-119
American Fork, Utah 84003
Kelsaybooks.com

To all of those out there still getting in good trouble, walking the walk, marching for our lives.

To my daughter Samantha, who I love beyond measure, and who I bet is tired of hearing me say yet again what a long strange trip it's been.

Acknowledgments

The author would like to thank the editors of the publications where versions of these poems first appeared, sometimes under different titles:

30 Poems in November: "To Look for America"
American Graveyard: Calls to End Gun Violence Vol 1: "My Opening Farewell: A Sonnet to Ten Days in March 2019"
American Graveyard: Calls to End Gun Violence Vol 2: "Dropping Off at the Cinema: The Dark Knight Rises," "Dylan's Mother Susan Klebold Gives a TED Talk," "He Fit the Profile," "R.I.P Jeremy Richman"
Cutthroat, A Journal of the Arts: "April 1999"
Ibbetson Street: "Ben, We Hardly Knew Ye" (nominated for Pushcart Prize 2023), "Robb Elementary School, Uvalde Texas," "The Turning," "Wayne Harris"
Joy Harjo Poetry Prize: "April 1999" (2022 finalist)
Merrimac Mic: Ten Years Gone: "18 and Overseas"
Poetry in Motion Festival 2024, Colorado Springs, Colorado: "April 1999"
Rattle: "When the phone rings"
Silkworm 14: "Practicing Tashlich: Linked Haibun"

Many poems in this collection began as drafts during a month I participated in the Tupelo Press 30/30 Project. Thanks as always to my brother Tom Wolf for his careful reading and honest feedback.

Contents

COLUMBINE HIGH SCHOOL

April 1999	15
Wayne Harris	18
Parenting in the Dark	20
What Are Your Aims in Raising a Child?	23
Rachel Joy Scott: A Chain of Kindness	24
Sammy Island	26
The Good Fairy of Wonder	28
Dylan's Mother Susan Klebold Gives a TED Talk	29
Ben, We Hardly Knew Ye	31
Dear Survivor	34

SANDY HOOK ELEMENTARY SCHOOL

Close Your Eyes, Hold Hands	37
The Turning	39
Dear Survivor	40
R.I.P Jeremy Richman	41
Moms Are Not a Magic Bullet	42
The Development of the Brain	44
A Letter in Which His Mother Is Mentioned	45
Dropping Off at the Cinema: The Dark Knight Rises	46
The Ogre Problem	48
The Cost of Lies, with Footnotes	49
When the phone rings	52
Mass Shootings Are Changing Us	54

MARJORY STONEMAN DOUGLAS HIGH SCHOOL

Parkland Florida: It Can Happen Here	57
18 and Overseas	59
'No Way To Prevent This,' Says Only Nation Where This Regularly Happens	60
To Look for America	61
He Fit the Profile	62
Dear Survivor	64
My Opening Farewell: A Sonnet to Ten Days in March 2019	65
Practicing Tashlich: Linked Haibun	67
Psychological Milestones	70

EPILOGUE

Still the Grass Grows	73
One night long ago and after dark	74
Robb Elementary School, Uvalde Texas	76

Notes	81
Further Reading	87
Poetry Anthologies	90
Further Action	91

COLUMBINE HIGH SCHOOL

April 20, 1999
15 dead, 24 injured

April 1999

My daughter was born the week after Columbine.

> My daughter was born new
> coated in creamy vernix, raw, startling:
> a gift, a challenge, a chance
> for a major do-over.

>> Trust yourself.
>> You know more than you think you do.
>> (*Dr. Spock's Baby and Child Care,* 7th Edition, p.1)

High schoolers. Trench coats. Crackling security films,
911 calls, voicemails to parents, kids
dripping out of windows. The taunts and screams
and all that blood.

> Blue blue eyes, tiny toes,
> wrinkly fingers splayed like starfish,
> patting my breast. Downy hair.
> Inked footprint on the birth announcement
> proclaiming our expanded family.

>> Every time you pick a baby up . . . every time you
>> change her, bathe her, feed her, smile at her,
>> she's getting the feeling that she belongs to you
>> and you belong to her. Nobody else in the world,
>> no matter how skillful, can give that to her.
>> (*Dr. Spock,* p.1–2)

They were bullied.
They were monsters.
Where were the parents.
It's the music, it's the price of
free love, it's the guns, it's
permissiveness, mental illness;
children with changed voices,
who three days prior danced at prom,
slaughtered, maimed,
traumatized.

    A friend gave me an archival box
    as a baby gift. A repository for the
    Sunday front page, weekly news magazines,
    grocery circulars, contemporary history,
    for the baby to appreciate as an adult.
    If she survived. I burned the printed pages,
    spread gray ash over bulbs planted the past fall.

        Raising children is more and more puzzling
        for many parents because we've lost a lot
        of our old-fashioned convictions about what kind
        of morals, ambitions, and character we want them
        to have. We are uncertain and worried about
        what kind of world awaits them as adults.
        (*Dr. Spock,* p.5)

We were all changed,
that week. We all wore
our cloak of perspective
just a little differently.

> Mothers are forever altered
> after giving birth. Deep down
> in their marrow, their bloodstream,
> the complex pinging patterns
> of their brains. My goal: to raise
> a worthy child, someone both
> strong and kind, who could outshine
> the bursts from the muzzle of a gun.

>> In many ways we have lost our faith in the meaning
>> of life and our confidence to understand our world
>> and our society.
>> (*Dr. Spock,* p.8)

Wayne Harris

called 911 on April 20th
and said the Columbine shooter
might be his son, Eric.

He said his son
was probably a part
of the Trench Coat Mafia.

Wayne Harris kept a journal
about his younger son, begun after
Eric had made a few bombs.

Maybe the garage smelled like
propane. Maybe it was just a parent's
intuition. The spidey sense tingling.

Eric had a beef with a boy at school
but his dad thought the other boy, Brooks,
was being dramatic. No big deal. Even though

Brooks reported death threats. On April 20th
Eric saw Brooks outside the school and said,
I like you now—stuff's about to go down-

you should leave. And Brooks booked it.
When he heard shots firing, Brooks
was the first person to call the police.

Maybe Wayne knew, as he filled his steno pad
with denial, maybe he knew something
was wrong—but before Columbine happened

it was hard to imagine Columbine. Maybe when
the police searched the Harris house that day
and found more bombs, evacuating the home

before the gunmen's bodies were identified-
Maybe that's when Wayne Harris knew
he made the right call.

Parenting in the Dark

Barks like a seal and whistling respiration:
the signature of croup. When my 2-year-old
called out in a raspy voice, I recognized the signs

overheard on a phone call with a colleague.
So I knew what to do. "Wow," I said. "It's the
middle of the night and you know what we need?

A steam bath!" And into the bathroom we went.
I turned the hot water on in the shower
while we sat snuggled on the toilet lid, singing

itsy-bitsy spider. Over and over and over. Because
a child with croup must be kept calm, in order
to breathe. A parent must project certainty.

We drew shapes on the steamed-up bathroom mirror.
When the hot water ran out, we put on jackets
and went out into the cold crisp air, the yellow dog

padding alongside me. I carried my toddler
around the block of townhouse condos, looking up
at the stars, wondering if the trees were friends

and did they play together in the dark? Back home,
I crawled into her bed, propping her tired body
up against mine, so she slept inclined, with mommy

right there to hear her breathe. In the morning
we saw the doctor, who confirmed the diagnosis
and the same home remedies. He patted my shoulder,

looked me in the eye and said: "Good luck, mom."
And so it went: fine by day, save a little sleepy,
barking by night. On the 3rd or 4th night comes a

croup crisis; the symptoms get worse. As we
sang that song again, that damn itsy-bitsy spider
still sliding down the spout, wondered as we walked

if the trees and bushes played together or if
they had separate games, like big kids and little kids,
I cursed the doctor. Was there nothing in the

21st-century toolkit more powerful than this?
Maybe steroids, or a nebulizer; my only child
fighting for breath, trusting me to take care of her.

What if I failed? This felt hopelessly old-fashioned.
Abe and Mary Lincoln probably used these same tricks.
And didn't their children die famously, and often?

And then the next morning, the croup was gone.
My child off chasing bubbles, laughing. I wondered
if I had imagined the whole thing, overreacted.

Until the next bout, every winter or fall,
all those preschool years. And each time
exactly like the first.

What Are Your Aims in Raising a Child?

So many parents get totally caught up in the difficult day-to-day issues of *how* they are parenting that they lose perspective about *why* they are parenting in the first place. I hope that raising your children will help you to understand your own ideas about what's *really* important to you in life and that this insight will guide the choices you make about raising your child.

—*Dr. Spock's Baby and Child Care,* p.6

Rachel Joy Scott: A Chain of Kindness

*What has happened to us as a people
that this should happen to us?*
   —Reverend Porter, at Rachel's funeral

Rachel left behind a trove of notes & messages,
drawings, a handprint behind a bureau, sparkly hearts.
Rachel wrote in her journal that she would die young.

Rachel, lunching outside with a friend that day,
was the first person shot at Columbine.
Her body remained outside the school overnight

alone with the stars, cool dew, and the abiding love
of her Lord and Savior. Rachel was a believer, not only
in God as the trinity of spirits, but also in our own

incarnation of love on earth. In an essay on ethics,
Rachel wrote: Compassion is the greatest form of
love humans have to offer. That is the message

that Rachel's family spreads, her words
more evocative than the things she left behind:
a white ivory casket, decorated with gratitude

and stunned grief; a red car, parked at the school,
transformed to a shrine; a young man, her brother,
who slammed a car door at her that morning,

before he saw his two best friends dragged out
from beside him, crouched and hiding, who heard
God's voice in his head, urging him to get up

and leave the library, while the shooters still
stormed the school, in the few moments it was
possible to escape. Craig Scott has consecrated

his own long life; decades after Rachel died
he retells her story: You never know how far
a little kindness can spread.

Sammy Island

After the fire, we lived for a spell
in a brown house in town, furnished
with other people's things. Later

we moved to an old converted schoolhouse
set on 4 acres which used to be the
town poor farm. It was haunted

but charming, with a broad front lawn
bordered by a stream feeding into the
Manhan River. My 4-year-old daughter

loved that yard. She and the yellow dog
would go exploring, toting a blue plastic bucket
and a hand-drawn treasure map. They collected

pinecones, luxurious swatches of moss, bits of
bird eggs, speckled stones, shed skin from snakes.
In shorts or bathing suits we would go

wading in the knee-deep stream. Just below
the backyard was a mud beach with a
fallen-branch bench and a clump of brush

around which the water diverged. It made
interesting currents for playing Pooh sticks.
One day my daughter and I were out wandering

and she got ahead of me, claiming the patch
we called Sammy Island. I loitered on the beach
thinking how fine it was to raise an independent girl

brave and curious, my own Rachel Carson, when she
called out "help mommy!" And in that instant,
I dropped my phone and plunged ahead in terror

cursing my carelessness, scourging myself for
ever taking my eyes off my one precious prize—
and then I found her, and the yellow dog,

tangled in a blackberry thicket, stained
in dark juice. "My shorts got stuckted,"
she said. "I think I tore them. Sorry, mommy."

As I laughed and gave thanks and hugged her
too tight she looked up at me, confused,
unsure if she should laugh or cry.

The Good Fairy of Wonder

If I had influence with the good fairy who is supposed to preside over the christening of all children, I should ask that her gift to each child in the world be a sense of wonder so indestructible that it would last throughout life, as an unfailing antidote against the boredom and disenchantments of later years, the sterile preoccupation with things that are artificial, the alienation from the sources of our strength.

—Rachel Carson, *The Sense of Wonder: A Celebration of Nature for Parents and Children*

Dylan's Mother Susan Klebold Gives a TED Talk

Sue Klebold says she did not know.
She asks herself if she was a terrible mother.
Sue Klebold loved her son.

Sue Klebold knows her son did a terrible thing,
for which she apologizes. She lives knowing
she might run into survivors anywhere she goes.

Two years before the Columbine shooting
Dylan wrote in a diary about cutting himself
and said that he wanted to die.

His mother did not know then but now
she sees that there was time to get him help
even though he did not ask.

There were no guns in the Klebold household.
Sue Klebold wants to know why it was so easy
for her troubled son to obtain so many guns

and why has this not changed
given all that we all know now
but did not know, back then.

Sue Klebold views Columbine
through the lens of her son's suicide.
She does not know when

Dylan's thoughts of suicide morphed
into plans for spectacular murder.
She says if love were enough,

there wouldn't be so many suicides.
Dylan Klebold and Eric Harris
are icons for mass murderers.

Their parents loved them.
But it was not enough.

Ben, We Hardly Knew Ye

Columbine Babies Reach High School, Fall 2014

Ben was a friend, a good friend,
who brought candy to sad girls.
He visited our house with his buds,

"the awkward boys." The kids played
Manhunt around town, which is like
Tag meets Capture the Flag (with kissing).

Ben made a Facebook page as Eric Harris.
He sent friend requests to all the gang.
My daughter had to ask who Eric Harris was

but she didn't tell me then that the boy
behind the page was Ben. She didn't want me
to worry. Or ban Ben from visiting the house.

The probation department in Littleton Colorado
said Eric Harris had the potential to do well in life
and was very intelligent.

The guidance department at our local high school
said the same about Ben. He had friends.
He tried out for the track team.

Ben was a wizard with video editing and computers.
He dubbed metallic music with reverberating screams into
Columbine security footage. No one told me that either.

We were on our way home from my in-laws
when my daughter got a call in the car
from a boy who was crying. It was about Ben.

My daughter had missed a call from Ben
the day before when she was at the movies.
Sometimes even kids miss calls.

But there was a voicemail.
From a very drunk Ben,
saying he loved her. He called

not long before he went to the ER
for alcohol poisoning; not long before
he was discharged against medical advice

went home with his hardworking father
and shot himself. The ambulance came
quickly and too late.

The sitting rooms at the wake were crowded
with choked-up parents and teachers, cradling
cider and seltzer water as if they were stiff drinks.

The porch was mobbed with mingling kids.
Pictures of Ben from the Homecoming Dance,
with my daughter, were out on display.

Parents kept asking the kids if Ben was bullied.
The police came to our house to listen to
the voicemail. They recorded the interview,

taking notes around the kitchen table.
A few hours later the local cop came back
with a state trooper, to talk about Columbine.

The cops were wondering if Ben was a potential
school shooter who succeeded only at suicide.
Six sophomore boys carried a coffin heavy with questions.

Ben was a sweet sassy awkward boy
fascinated by guns, Eric Harris,
and Dylan Klebold.

Ben died at 15
leaving behind many broken hearts,
a ragged tear in the fabric of the world.

Dear Survivor

One of the hardest things you need to know about losing someone to a mass shooting is that you might not get to say goodbye. You need to remember that they loved you no matter what. No matter how many fights you had, or if you didn't say I love you enough, they know you did. Life changes when somebody dies, and your view of the world shifts.

You can see the best and the worst of people. You'll never be the same, but you'll learn to live with this.

—Excerpt, a letter written to future survivors of mass shootings by Jazmin Cazares, 17. Jazmin's 9-year-old sister Jackie was killed in the shooting at Robb Elementary School in Uvalde, Texas, May 24, 2022.

SANDY HOOK ELEMENTARY SCHOOL

December 14, 2012
28 dead, 2 injured

Close Your Eyes, Hold Hands

By any measure, we are failing these children.
    —Barack Obama, Newtown CT

The first person he killed that morning
was his mother. In her home, in her bed,
shot 4 times in the head.

Adam Lanza took his mother's car to
Sandy Hook Elementary School, where
he shot and killed 20 first-grade students
plus 6 adults, including the principal. Then
Adam shot himself.

There was controversy over how many
crosses to erect. Someone put out 28
but 2 crosses were torn down.

It's easy, it's common, it's practically protocol
to blame the mother. Nancy Lanza, after all,
bought the guns. Nancy Lanza brought her son
to shooting ranges. It was something they did
together. Mother and son, son and mother
    but he had problems with women
mother trying to care for son
    refused to talk to his dad
mother moving only as directed in her own house
    he's down cellar playing his games
trying to help, trying to get him services, trying, trying
    he's going through a tough time

Adam left behind a massive spreadsheet
of mass murders, videos from Columbine,

and selfies posed holding a gun to his head.

Adam's father Peter, interviewed two years after,
is haunted every hour of every day. All those children.
All their parents. All 4 bullets in his ex-wife; one trigger-pull
for each member of the Lanza family.

Peter Lanza wishes his own second son
had never been born.

The Turning

On the day the babies died
President Obama said to hug your children
And he cried.

On the day the babies died
My baby was in middle school,
Working as an intern at the
After School Program for grades
K—6. When she arrived at work
Teachers were crying. They had
Twenty minutes to get ready.

That afternoon the school was in
Lockdown: Adult supervisors at the
Outside doors, college staff in the
Hallways, interns in a ring around the
Little kids, all gathered together
Inside a cleared-out cafeteria;
My 13-year-old's body
The last barrier between
These babies
And a bullet.

Dear Survivor

My form of guilt came from the inability to hug my mom and dad. It wasn't that I felt like they "didn't get" it or they "didn't understand". It was because there were other parents out there that would never hug their children again. I felt guilty for receiving love and comfort and I wish that someone would have told me, it is OK to hug your loved ones. Hold each other tight because love and comfort are going to be a huge part of your recovery process. "The greatest gift you'll ever learn is to love and be loved in return."

—Excerpt, a letter written to future survivors of mass shootings by Missy Mendo, survivor of Columbine

R.I.P Jeremy Richman

Why would someone walk into a school and kill my child?
I need to know that answer.
—Jennifer Hensel, mother of Avielle Richman

Jeremy Richman looked for patterns
deep inside the structures of the brain.
In the prefrontal cortex, site of planning
and decisions, weighing of consequences.
In the limbic system, the triad of structures
concerned with triaging emotions:
      fear   hunger   anger
guilt   shame   anxiety
learning shaping biological responses
shaping learning, in a cycle which iterates
& iterates   & iterates.

How does it diverge
                                    into violence?

His hypothesis: long-range, humans survived
by building bonds. What must go wrong
for a grown man to aim a weapon of war
into the face of a child?

Jeremy Richman believed
we would find this answer
lurking in the blob of a brain.
He needed to honor his daughter,
Avielle, who died at Sandy Hook.
He used every tool that he had
trudging through the toughest mud
until he found that he couldn't
endure another day.

Moms Are Not a Magic Bullet

When she smashed the screen of our daughter's iPod
my ex-husband called his girlfriend "passionate".

When she scheduled manicures, massages, & weekends away
on visit nights, dad dinners, or opening nights of plays

he rescheduled or ghosted our girl. I made a new rule:
over 30 minutes late with no call canceled the visit.

When she yelled and threw things as our daughter hid
huddled in the guest bathroom, the therapist suggested

we all come in for a big group counseling session.
I vetoed that. His girlfriend didn't play any part

in my parenting plan. They broke up, a few times;
were arrested for domestic assault, a few times;

failed to attend meetings or follow the program.
So instead, I got an order barring the girlfriend

from being in the presence of my girl. I slid into court
during one of the months they lived apart, when he

(briefly) had his own place. I'm good with logistics.
Harder to handle was when my twelve-year-old—

who had recorded a ringtone saying "this is your
awesome daughter calling"—sat sobbing in the corner

of our big brown comfy couch, barely able to breathe.
"Why don't they like me?" she asked.

"What is wrong with me, and why did my dad
choose her instead?"

The Development of the Brain

Rich, emotionally positive experiences tend to promote certain complex brain connections. Negative experiences also reinforce certain connections in the brain, although perhaps not the ones we would like to see . . .

—Dr. Spock's Baby and Child Care, p.20

A Letter in Which His Mother Is Mentioned

IN REFERENCE to nearly every news report and newspaper article about **the Newtown massacre**, I want to remind everyone that there were more than 26 people killed. I understand why the shooter Adam Lanza's suicide is rarely mentioned, but **his mother was the first person he killed.**

As a mother myself, I am amazed that her death is rarely mentioned. Their family will be grieving the death of two family members, and bearing the weight of what Lanza did.

Tinka Perry
Mansfield
The Boston Globe, Dec 29, 2012

Dropping Off at the Cinema:
The Dark Knight Rises

It was a July night, not too steamy, but humid enough
that the popcorn smell from the theater hunkered down
in the scruffy parking lot, by crushed soda cups and
tattered candy wrappers. We pulled up under a light,
moderately far from the entrance, to avoid embarrassment.
The girls popped out, checked their outfits
(did they not plan these by phone, and also coordinate
hair and make-up?). We ran the checklist: phones, water,
wallets. We transferred K's bag to my car.

Off they went. We moms lingered, chatting. Watching
the girls enter the cinema, I stopped, trying to focus
at a distance, in the dark. "Wait," I asked. "Is that a car
dropping off, or a cab, or a cop?" We stared.
It was definitely a cop. Just sitting there.

Huh. It slowly dawned on us a dozen people were killed
in Colorado, and 70 more hurt, watching this same movie,
two days ago. I wondered, out loud but unsure,
"What do you think? Are they responding to a threat,
or just showing they care?"

"I'm sure it's nothing," my friend said. "A precaution, is all."

"You're probably right," I said. Neither of us moved.

We stared some more. We were on unstable ground now.
I turned back to my friend, who had another kid and a husband
and a glass of wine awaiting her at home. "Tell you what,"

I said. "I don't have to leave right away. I'll just hang here
and make sure it's nothing. When I feel silly or get bored,
I'll go home. If anything happens, I'll grab both kids
and hightail it to your house."

"You sure?" she asked. "Want me to stay?"

"I feel kind of stupid staying myself," I said. "No need for
both of us to stand here. You go ahead. I'll head out soon."

We hugged, awkwardly. She left. I kept staring
at the cop car still parked by the entrance
for 20–30 minutes. Maybe more. Until I was sure
the ads were over and the movie had begun and still
nothing had happened. No copycats here.

Later I went back to get the girls, who happily babbled
about the movie, and who else was there, and who
wasn't there with them, and all the other things
kids talk about when they're not preoccupied with
tear gas grenades and gunmen
and getting massacred in the dark.

The Ogre Problem

It is not your job as a parent to banish all fears from your child's imagination. In fact, learning to face and conquer one's fears is an important lesson. Your job is to help your child learn constructive ways to cope with and conquer those fears. In the eloquent words of Selma Fraiberg in *The Magic Years*: "The future mental health of the child does not depend on the presence or absence of ogres in his fantasy life. It depends on the child's solution to the ogre problem."

—Dr. Spock's Baby and Child Care, p.284–285

The Cost of Lies, with Footnotes[1]

Proceedings to consider damages, defamation lawsuit
against Alex Jones, August 2022

ALEX JONES, the day of the Sandy Hook shooting, Infowars:
"It's more than these dead poor children—
    you've gotta go with your gut,
        and my gut tells me
            I've never felt this freaked out . . .   I really think
                they're going to come after our guns
                      and start a civil war . . .
Don't ever think
    the globalists who hijacked this country
        wouldn't stage something like this.
            They kill little kids all day, every day."[2]

SCARLETT LEWIS, mother of Jesse Lewis, 6 years old, murdered in his first-grade classroom:
"Jesse was real. I'm a real mom."[3]

ALEX JONES, Infowars, March 2014
"Folks, we've got video of Anderson Cooper
      with clear blue-screen out there . . .
           He's not there in the town square.

---

[1] *From the closing argument by attorney Kyle Farrar: "Speech is free, but you have to pay for your lies." Proceedings to consider damages against Alex Jones, Travis County Courthouse, Austin TX, August 2022*

[2] *On December 14, 2012, 26 students and teachers at Sandy Hook Elementary School and 2 members of the Lanza family were shot and killed by Adam Lanza. For real.*

[3] *Scarlett Lewis excerpts from testimony at the proceedings to consider damages against Alex Jones 8/2022*

We got people clearly coming up and laughing and then
    doing the fake crying. We've clearly got people where
        it's actors playing different parts for different people,
            the building bulldozed, covering up everything . .

SCARLETT LEWIS, mother of Jesse, who bravely told other kids to run when the gun jammed:
"The fear and anxiety and unsafeness . . . keeps me from healing,"

Sept 2014: InfoWars publishes "FBI SAYS NO ONE KILLED AT SANDY HOOK." [4]

ALEX JONES, Infowars, Dec 2014:
"The whole thing is a giant hoax . . .
    The general public doesn't know
        the school was actually closed the year before.
      They don't know they've sealed it all,
        demolished the building.
They don't know that they had the kids going in circles
    in and out of the building as a photo-op . . . .
        But it took me about a year with Sandy Hook
      to come to grips with the fact
        that the whole thing was fake."

NEIL HESLIN, father of Jessie Lewis, who described holding his son's bullet-ridden body in his arms, on national television, on Father's Day, regarding Alex Jones' absence from court:

---

[4] *This article has been removed*

"My life has been threatened. I fear for my life.
I fear for my safety and my family's safety and their life . . .
Mr. Alex Jones does not have the courage to face me." [5]

ALEX JONES, Infowars, Dec 2014:
I mean, I couldn't believe it . . . .
    But then I did deep research—
        and my gosh, it just pretty much didn't happen."

SCARLETT LEWIS, testifying with Alex Jones sitting in the courtroom:
"Truth is so vital in our world . . . Sandy Hook is a hard truth. Hard truth. Nobody would want to ever believe that 26 kids could be murdered."

ALEX JONES, taped deposition, for a defamation lawsuit brought by multiple Sandy Hook families Mar 2019:
        "And I, myself, have almost had like
  a form of psychosis   back in the past
        where I basically thought
          everything was staged, even though
      I'm now learning   a lot of times
            things aren't staged."[6]

---

[5] *Neil Heslin excerpt from testimony at the proceedings to consider damages against Alex Jones 8/2022*

[6] *WTAF*

When the phone rings

while you're visiting your father,
and I know it's you because
it's your ringtone, the notes in a tune
you chose, so it would be bright and
I would know it was you, and
answer my phone, so it's a sound
both buoyant and urgent, it's a
need in three notes, and while I wish
you weren't visiting your father,
since it upsets you when you do, there's
always some part of the story you'll
tell me that's off, that raises an
alarm, a flag, but after all this time
we don't need subtle clues, do we,
we know he's not right, so is it wise
to visit him again but in the back
of our minds is the night he was so
stoned on the phone and then dead
on the men's room floor—
      but they brought him back—
and so you go, again, to his new
sober living apartment because what if

next time he is gone, what if, and so
you go visit and I answer the ringing phone
for you to tell me you hiked up a hill
so high you saw all the way to Boston and
there were clouds reflected in the glass
of the Hancock building, like the blue sky
was both solid as a tower and as
gossamer as hope and anyway
you are on the road and your
favorite artist just dropped an album
so you need me to stay off our shared
Spotify so you can sing out loud
all the way home.

Mass Shootings Are Changing Us

They happen so fast now that there isn't even time to have the gun control argument in full; we have it in a barrage of angry tweets and then brace for the next one. It all plays out like a familiar haiku:

My hopes and prayers
Too soon, mental health, too soon
Hopes and prayers, guns, guns

—Dahlia Lithwick, *Slate.com*

MARJORY STONEMAN DOUGLAS HIGH SCHOOL

February 14, 2018
17 dead, 17 injured

Parkland Florida:
It Can Happen Here

He looked like a typical high school student,
and for a quick moment I thought,
'Could this be the person who I need to stop?
—The officer that arrested the Parkland shooter

Does it matter if his mother is dead or in jail? Was the damage
already done, in the time they shared the alcohol in her blood
and the bits from her own bones that make up his body?
The lawyers argue over PET scans of his brain, what they do
or don't show; the lawyers argue over the doctors who
argue over words and what they mean. No one argues
that Nikolas Cruz walked into that school with a long gun
and hundreds of bullets, that next came 4 long minutes
when he fired and fired and fired and fired
    on the first floor on the second floor on the next floor
        in the hallways in the classrooms into closets into corners
            bullets bullets blood blood
                bullets bullets and blood
so many fragments of bone, so many texts and calls to
mom and dad, to brothers and sisters, so many fractured lives.
Despite all we knew about him before that Valentine's Day,
a day for red hearts, red roses, flowery poems; after
so very many red flag red flag red flag moments missed
here's yet another kid with another AR-15 and another
hashtag placename, yet another site where families gathered,
where officers entered after agonizing hours to announce:
There are no more survivors left at the scene.
No more survivors.   So if you are still here waiting . . .

    (the wall of sound travels for blocks
        anguished wails and bellowing screams
            as one by one   parents understand   exactly
              what it means   to have a child   who didn't
                        survive   )

We are all still there, balanced in that chasm
between before and after; we are all still watching
X Gonzalez stand at the mic in silence for the
4 excruciating minutes of slaughter out of the
6 minutes and 20 seconds they spent on stage
and the shooter spent rampaging in the Parkland school.
We are all on scene, we are all marching
for our lives, shouting atop of cars, and yet
somewhere out there, blending into the crowd
of careless, laughing, dancing people
of terrorized, bleeding, fleeing people
is the next Nikolas Cruz.

18 and Overseas

My daughter was taking a gap year at the time of the Parkland shooting. My daughter split her senior year of high school between community college classes and an internship working with the homeless; she spent Fridays and Saturdays serving sandwiches in the park and dinner at a café. My daughter bodysurfed at emo/screamo concerts. She sometimes said yes and sometimes said no. My daughter is 5'7" with vibrant dyed hair and a wolf tattooed on her left bicep. Her father is an addict who spent time in jail; her mother is a protester who writes poetry. On Valentine's Day 2018 my daughter was an au pair in China, getting a 4-year-old to school on a motorbike through Shanghai morning rush hour. My daughter planned to go from there to volunteer at an orphanage in Accra Ghana. People asked me, do you think that she is safe? and I clapped back, honestly, do you think she is safe here?

> freckle-faced boys
> with AR-15s
> American as apple pie

'No Way To Prevent This,' Says Only Nation Where This Regularly Happens

Published February 14, 2018: *The Onion*

PARKLAND, FL—In the hours following a violent rampage in Florida in which a lone attacker killed 17 individuals and seriously injured over a dozen others, citizens living in the only country where this kind of mass killing routinely occurs reportedly concluded Wednesday that there was no way to prevent the massacre from taking place. "This was a terrible tragedy, but sometimes these things just happen and there's nothing anyone can do to stop them," said Indiana resident Harold Turner, echoing sentiments expressed by tens of millions of individuals who reside in a nation where over half of the world's deadliest mass shootings have occurred in the past 50 years and whose citizens are 20 times more likely to die of gun violence than those of other developed nations. "It's a shame, but what can we do? There really wasn't anything that was going to keep this individual from snapping and killing a lot of people if that's what they really wanted." At press time, residents of the only economically advanced nation in the world where roughly two mass shootings have occurred every month for the past eight years were referring to themselves and their situation as "helpless."

To Look for America

I look up to heaven only when I want to sneeze.
—Ivan Turgenev, *Fathers and Sons*

In the olden days
we learned Stop, Drop, and Roll.
We knew the dance was ending
with the last chance to stand close and sway
when they played Stairway to Heaven.

Now the kids learn
RUN. HIDE. FIGHT.
They know the lockdown is over
when they leave the building, escorted,
hands over heads or on each other's shoulders
while some joker's phone plays Pumped Up Kicks.

He Fit the Profile

White man, toting a black bag.
Kinda unkempt. In a room where
he didn't belong (Philosophy of Ethics,
PH 3021), sitting next to me
checking out my tree-of-life tattoo,
pawing at my streaked purple hair.
Oily-ass smile, sitting oddly at an
angle, obstructing the only door.
Others catch the creepy vibe,
move slowly closer to the
trash can, fire extinguisher,
any possible projectile;
open the window, try to spy
security or staff passing by.
The teacher came in, nodded,
allowed a stranger to remain
(she's a stranger here herself,
from Austria? Russia?), opened
her laptop, class discussion.
We started typing goodbyes
into our phones
(I love you mom)
hidden under the desks.
Do we hit send? Save to notes?
Will we have time?

Then he started talking,
called a girl the n-word,
wouldn't shut up,
wouldn't leave. The teacher
finally threatens to call the cops

and he bolts. *WTF,* we ask,
what took you so long? We are
tweaking now. *Why didn't you
throw that dude out right away?
Call the code? Go to lockdown?*

The teacher is totally confused.
Why didn't you say something,
she asks. *Speak up. Act out.
How was I to know he was a threat?*

That's not how it works!! I yell
ready to rumble now that he's not
breathing in my space. *We're
supposed to DE-escalate.
Remain calm, distract,
peg the exits. Run for cover.
He fit the profile of a shooter.
What was in that bag?
How many guns? How many bullets?
No more teddy-bear shrines.
We're just kids.
We just wanna live.*

Dear Survivor

I hope none of you ever have to feel the adrenaline rush of fleeing from a school building you consider home because gunshots now ring throughout the halls.

I hope you never have to experience waiting in a parking lot down the street from your school, not knowing whether your friends or teachers or siblings or cousins are going to make it to that parking lot.

—Excerpt, a letter written to future survivors of mass shootings by Bryanna Love, survivor of the 2022 shooting at St. Louis Central Visual & Performing Arts High School in St. Louis, Missouri

My Opening Farewell:
A Sonnet to Ten Days in March 2019

1. Zoom down to the precision of a properly packed cartridge: the primer, the propellant, the bullet; the nip of air; the burn. Kinetic energy= ½ mass x velocity^2. How do we measure the effect, over time and space? 2. On 15 March a white man with many weapons exited his car. Saying "Let's get this party started," he broadcast live on Facebook. Footage of the massacre in a mosque was mirrored to YouTube. Videos were uploaded/ blocked/ uploaded/ blocked over 1.5 million times. 3. Live footage, of people at prayer, slaughtered, with narration. 4. The reddit r/watchpeopledie was taken offline. Jews from the Tree of Life Synagogue in Pittsburgh began fundraising for the Muslims of Christchurch New Zealand. 5. That same day a husband and wife were killed at home in Alton NH. Both were shot once in the head. The couple homeschooled their three children, including twin 11-year-old boys. 6. An 11-year-old was arrested for the crime. He was not publicly identified by police, but the Community Church of Alton is praying for his soul. 7. An Indiana teachers' union tweeted that teachers were taken in groups of four and shot execution style, with a pellet gun, as part of an active shooter training. In photos the teachers appeared bloodied and bruised. 8. Two days later a young woman from Parkland, who graduated from Marjory Stoneman Douglas High without her best friend, shot herself in the head. 9. The Facebook account for the Women's March posted the tragedy. The headline read "committed suicide" instead of

"died by suicide." Over one hundred people called out that error in the comments. 10. Six days later a young man from Parkland, a sophomore at Marjory Stoneman Douglas High, died by suicide. 11. On March 25 the father of a first grader killed at Sandy Hook Elementary, a father since devoted to studying brain health and violence, was discovered at the town hall in Newtown, dead by suicide. 12. Boomers say, that would never happen here. Not in our town. This is not who we are. 13. The kids say, this is the event we have been training for our entire lives. 14. Long ago, in a speech about the challenge of reaching the moon, JFK declared technology has no conscience of its own. The same could be said of terminal ballistics: the study of a projectile impacting a target and the lethality of wounds.

Practicing Tashlich: Linked Haibun

1.

River mud makes me happy. In the summer of covid I take frequent walks with the dog. I look for trails where we can wade into rivers or streams, moving water without the green algae bloom, where I can see fish, frogs leaping, freshwater clams. The summer our house burned down I took my toddler daughter and dog to a canoe take-out on a river bend, behind a farmer's corn field. The dog fetched sticks over and over. My daughter made piles of mud topped with stones we called Yertle the Turtle. She chose a stick or a rock or a clamshell and told it stories. "My house was on fire," she said. "The smoke made everything yucky and my toys are all gone." Wake from passing boats toppled her tower.

cute little white girls
look to police as helpers
to keep us all safe.

2.

After we split up my husband flamed out. Rehab released rage long buried, numbed by substances. At night before bed my daughter insisted I walk through the house to check all the doors and windows were locked. "He must have threatened to get me in my sleep," I joked to a friend. "Maybe," she replied. "But write it all down. A change in behavior is evidence of trauma." I tracked every missed call, every missed visit, every red-hot email that made it through the firewall. My daughter disclosed to therapists instead of muddy sticks. Her dad said he would kill me. Her dad said he would kidnap her, cut her hair, change her name. I went to court with bulging files seeking orders of protection. My daughter did not testify: I did. Cross-examination was like crawling naked through a minefield laid by an ex-lover, in public, questions and objections hurled like incoming grenades. After each battle I took my daughter to the ocean at sunset, fiery orange hues spreading over waves.

evidence is stored
in many different forms
tears. nightmares. long bones.

3.

This year my daughter turned 21. She took an extra job, moved to a bigger apartment, covered a hole behind the stove with tinfoil to deter bats. The foil blocks their sonar, she tells me. So the bats can't tell the wall is compromised. Her red hair is streaked with blue. She worries about everyone's safety, swaps masks to match her outfits, socializes solely within a small pod. It is the summer of covid. Her father has completed a jail sentence and several stints of rehab. My daughter and I spend a few days away, climbing rocks on a secluded state beach. We take turns telling stories. I listen. I learn things. She can legally order drinks, prefers them sweet, layered with chocolate liqueurs. We laugh. Heading back to the hotel we skip rocks across the water, casting off our cares.

on the fertile banks
of a broad sturdy river
mud leaches out trauma.

Psychological Milestones

A central problem for adolescents and young adults is to find out or investigate what kind of people they are going to be, doing what work, living by what principles. This is partly a conscious, but even more an unconscious, process . . . In groping to find this identity adolescents may try out a variety of roles: dreamer, cosmopolitan, cynic, leader of lost causes, ascetic, and so on . . . The eventual outcome will be influenced by 3 circumstances: the extent of their dependency, the intensity of their rebelliousness and rivalry, and the kind of outside world they live in and what it asks of them.

—*Dr. Spock's Baby and Child Care,* p.313–314

EPILOGUE

Still the Grass Grows

. . . almost every community that we'd gone to where something horrible had happened, they all had dead grass around them because of the thousands of people that come in and stand on it and ask for justice, ask for peace, and might get some temporary answer. But then eventually, that grass comes back just to die again.

—David Hogg, 19, survivor of the shooting at Marjory Stoneman Douglas High School, Parkland, Florida

One night long ago and after dark

we were walking in circles
wider, smaller, the same, I don't know
because we were lost, or rather the car
was lost, because I couldn't remember
exactly where I parked. There are many
lots along Route 1, leading to the
Topsfield Fair, and we've been there so long,
rode so many dizzying rides and petted
so many animals. Now we were ready
to go home, if only we could find
our beloved Toyota. My daughter and I
and her current best friend trudged along
with less and less good humor. I clicked
the remote to see if any car winked at us
but none of them did. "We should call
my dad," said the friend. "He'll know."
We look at her. "OK," I said, "we can call
but he wasn't with us, so how would
he know where we parked?"
"Dads know," she said, "they just do."
Then she looked at my daughter. "Well
maybe not all dads," she said. "I mean
the dads that care. I mean,"
she went on, trying not to be mean,
"maybe I should shut up now."

"How about if we ask one of the
nice parking people," I said.
"Maybe they can help. We know our
plate number. They're already here."
My daughter looked at me.
So far no one was crying.

"It's OK," I said, taking each girl's hand,
"we got this. We'll be home
before the carriage turns to a pumpkin
and the horses back into mice."

"Mom," my daughter said, rolling her eyes,
"you said we could watch a movie.
With subtitles, to sing along.
And can we still make cookies?"

"Of course", I said. "First, home.
And then, cookies."

A nice parking lot man
drove us around in a cart
until finally my clicker
flashed our friendly headlights
and we headed for home.

Looking back, I reckon
the girls had just started fourth grade.

Robb Elementary School, Uvalde Texas

May 24 2022: 21 dead, 17 injured

After Chris Llewellyn

It was Tuesday. School was out
in two days. It started before noon.
Most of the dead and wounded
were ten years old.

He bought the gun
legally
the day after he turned
eighteen. He was known to
torture small animals.
He posted threats online.
                It was Tuesday.

There was an award ceremony at school
that morning. Many parents attended.
Some kids wanted to go home after
but most stayed for bubbles and
class parties.
              School was out in two days.

He called his mother a bitch
and moved in with his grandmother.
He shot his grandmother in the face
that morning, stole her truck, and drove
to his old elementary school.
              It started before noon.

There were fences. There were locks.
There were police officers.
They had training. They had drills.
The officers were armed.
                Most of the dead and wounded
                were ten years old.

The gunman entered the school with an AR-15
and lots of ammunition.
                It was Tuesday.

The gunman entered two adjoining
fourth grade classrooms. In one room,
every student died. The teacher was shot
multiple times.
                School was out in two days.

For over an hour law enforcement officers
converged in the hallway. Hundreds of
law enforcement officers. For over an hour.
The officers had guns. The officers
had shields.
                It started before noon.

Some of the victims bled out
while officers stood in the hall.
The survivors played dead.
Some of the children covered themselves
in the blood of their classmates.
                      Most of the dead and wounded
                      were ten years old.

It was 23 years after Columbine.
It was 10 years after Sandy Hook.
It was 4 years after Parkland.
                      It was Tuesday.

Notes

"April 1999"—The Columbine sections of the poem are based on the *Wikipedia* article Columbine High School massacre; a *Denver Post* article "Officials think bombs at Columbine High School were planted during prom" from April 24, 1999; a *Time* article "The Littleton Massacre: . . . in Sorrow And Disbelief" published May 3, 1999; a Newsweek "Rewind: 15 Years After Columbine, a Nation Still Asks 'Why?'" from April 17, 2014; and a *Washington Post* retrospective "Bullies and black trench coats: The Columbine shooting's most dangerous myths" published April 19, 2019.

—*Dr. Spock's Baby and Child Care* 7th Edition c. 1998 was my bible when I had my daughter. Our home burned down when she was 3. This was the first book I replaced.

—The section on mothers' bodies being altered by pregnancy is based on NPR reporting on microchimerism: "Fetal Attraction" from May 2, 2012 and "Fetal Cells May Protect Mom From Disease Long After The Baby's Born" from Oct 26, 2015.

"Wayne Harris"—This poem was based on the general Columbine sources plus "Eric Harris' Parents & Brother, Wayne, Kathy & Kevin Harris: 5 Fast Facts You Need to Know" published on heavy.com April 2019.

"Rachel Joy Scott: A Chain of Kindness"—Sources for this poem include the *Wikipedia* article on Rachel Scott, Rachel's "About" page on the Rachel's Challenge website, and the *Denver Post* "Victim's legacy grows at youth rally" August 8, 1999.

"The Good Fairy of Wonder"—The Rachel Carson quote is from her book *The Sense of Wonder: A Celebration of Nature for Parents and Children,* 1965. The book was published shortly after Carson's death. I read it when my daughter was young, and it inspired many outdoor adventures.

"Dylan's Mother Susan Klebold Gives a TED Talk"—This poem was based on the general Columbine sources plus a Colorado Public Radio segment "'I'll Never Know If I Could Have Prevented It,' Says Mother Of Columbine Shooter" from Feb 16, 2016. The TED talk "My son was a Columbine shooter. This is my story" from November 2016 has over 25 million views on TED and YouTube combined.

"Dear Survivor"—On the 10th anniversary of the Sandy Hook shooting, December 14 2022, Good Morning America asked dozens of school shooting survivors across multiple incidents to write letters to survivors of future incidents. Specifically, they were asked to let future survivors know what to expect and share what they wish they had known earlier in their own journey. The letters are online at: abcnews.go.com/GMA/News/dear-future-survivor-school-shooting-survivors-pen-letters/story?id=93887965.

"Close Your Eyes, Hold Hands"—The title of this poem is the instruction that was given to children as they were being escorted out of the Sandy Hook Elementary School. Sources for information on the shooting and the Lanza family are "Report finds missed chances to help Newtown shooter Adam Lanza" from CNN on November 21, 2014 and "The Reckoning" from the *New Yorker* on March 17, 2014. There's a long look at President Obama's reaction to the Sandy Hook shooting on History.com including the quote used as an epigraph and the advice to hug your children: www.history.com/the-obama-years/newtown.html.

"The Turning"—President Obama's reaction to the Sandy Hook shooting is above.

"R. I. P. Jeremy Richman"—Sources for this poem include "Sandy Hook's tragic legacy: seven years on, a loving father is the latest victim" from *The Guardian* on March 31, 2019 and "Before his suicide, Sandy Hook dad and neuroscientist sought origins of violence in the brain" from CNN, April 4, 2019. The Guardian article is where I learned about the extreme marathon event Tough Mudder and the Mud for Brains team which raised funds for the Avielle Foundation.

"A Letter in Which His Mother Is Mentioned"—This is an erasure poem based on a Letter to the Editor published in *The Boston Globe* on December 29, 2012.

"Dropping Off at the Cinema: The Dark Knight Rises"—This poem refers to a shooting at a movie theater in Aurora, Colorado on July 20, 2012. More information can be found at the ABC News article "A look back at the Aurora, Colorado, movie theater shooting 5 years later" published July 20, 2017.

"The Cost of Lies, With Footnotes[1]"—This is basically a found poem combining material from different sources. The Alex Jones quotes are from *First Amendment Watch* "Deep Dive: Alex Jones and the Sandy Hook Defamation Suits" and a *NY Daily News* article "A Look At Alex Jones Decade of Deceit on Sandy Hook," published on August 5, 2022. The Scarlett Lewis quotes are from a *Today* article "Sandy Hook Mom Scarlett Lewis Confronts Alex Jones In Court" (accessed via Yahoo news) from August 2, 2022 or from CBS News on August 3, 2022, "Mother of 6-year-old killed in Sandy Hook takes witness stand and confronts Alex Jones about his lies: "My son existed." Neil Heslin's quotes are from an August 2 *Austin American-Statesman* article, "Alex Jones trial: Parent says hoax portrayal turned life into a 'living hell'." The idea for a footnote poem came from a workshop given during the Tupelo Press 30/30 project that same month.

"Mass Shootings Are Changing Us"—The Dahlia Lithwick quote is from a *Slate* article of the same title from December 4, 2015, found at slate.com/news-and-politics/2015/12/mass-shootings-are-changing-us-lockdowns-guns-and-fear.html.

"Parkland Florida: It Can Happen Here"—General information on the shooting and the gunman are sourced from the History.com article "Teen gunman kills 17, injures 17 at Parkland, Florida high school" (where the epigraph quote appears) and an AP article from October 3, 2022 "Florida school shooter contemplated massacre for years." The description of the speech is from *The Cut*, published March 24, 2018: "Emma González's March for Our Lives Speech Lasted As Long As the Parkland Shooting." "[S]houting atop of cars" refers to an image of Cameron Kasky, an MSD student who co-founded Never Again MSD, speaking on top of a car. The photo was a throwback to an image of Mario Savio from the Berkeley Free Speech Movement standing on top of a police car in 1964.

"'No Way to Prevent This,' Says Only Nation Where This Regularly Happens"—*The Onion*, a satirical news website, reprints this article with the place and casualty numbers changed for mass shooting events involving 10 or more deaths. Between May 2014 and October 2023 the article was reprinted 36 times. The original author Jason Roeder lived less than a mile from Marjory Stoneman Douglas High School at the time of the Parkland shooting. www.theonion.com/no-way-to-prevent-this-says-only-nation-where-this-r-1823016659

"To Look for America"—The title refers to the chorus of Simon and Garfunkel's song *America*. *Stairway to Heaven* was released by Led Zeppelin in 1971. The third stanza of the poem is based on an amazing *This American Life* segment "Kids These Days, Act One: This Is Not A Drill" which aired October 28, 2022. *Pumped Up Kicks* is by Foster the People, released in 2011.

"He Fit the Profile"—The actions taken by students who thought there was a potential gunman in their classroom are included in an active shooter tips brochure provided to schools by the FBI: www.fbi.gov/how-we-can-help-you/active-shooter-safety-resources. American public-school students really do train for these events all their lives.

"My Opening Farewell: A Sonnet to Ten Days in March 2019"— All of the events referenced in this poem actually occurred, in the sequence given, and were reported in local New England news or the *Washington Post*. The suicides of 3 mass shooting survivors is discussed in an ABC News article from March 27, 2019 "Suicides highlight mass shooting survivors' trauma and fragility of healing: 'We still live with it every day." The format of the poem is an homage to "Sonnet, with Pride" by Sherman Alexie, which appeared in the *Best American Poetry 2014* anthology. The discussion of the properties of a cartridge was reviewed with a hunter and sports shooter who happened to be having lunch at a pizza place near my office while I was revising this poem.

"Practicing Tashlich: Linked Haibun"—Tashlich is a Jewish atonement ritual, usually performed on the High Holy Day of Rosh Hashanah, where sins are cast out upon flowing water. In our town people throw bits of bread into the Merrimack River.

"Still the Grass Grows"—This quote was taken from an interview featured in the *Washington Post Magazine* on June 25, 2019 titled "Parkland's David Hogg: Children having to go through active shooter drills is not what freedom looks like to me." David Hogg is a co-founder of March for Our Lives and Leaders We Deserve.

"Robb Elementary School, Uvalde Texas"—The basic facts of this shooting are included in the article "An American Girl" from the *Washington Post,* a profile of then 10-year-old survivor Caitlyne Gonzales, published on October 24, 2022. I have not yet read this article without crying. The format of the poem is homage to the anchor poem of the collection *Fragments from the Fire: The Triangle Shirtwaist Company Fire of March 25, 1911* by Chris Llewellyn, originally published in 1987.

Further Reading

This is not a comprehensive bibliography, but what stayed with me after preparing for this project.

—Elizabeth S. Wolf

"After a toddler accidentally shot and killed his older sister, a family's wounds run deep." *Washington Post,* December 1, 2016. An in-depth portrait of a horrifically common occurrence in a country awash with guns.

"The children haunted by 12 seconds of gunfire." *The Week,* June 25, 2017. "A meaningful number of those kids are going to have significant struggles," said Bruce Perry, a psychiatrist who worked with families from Columbine and Sandy Hook. "It's stunning how one event can have this echo that will impact so many more individuals than people realized."

"Sandy Hook Parents Sue Alex Jones for Defamation." *Outside the Beltway,* April 27, 2018. An overview of the Sandy Hook parents' civil actions against Alex Jones of Infowars. The parents prevailed in court in 2022 and were taking actions to collect as in 2024–2025.

"The fear we all live with." *The Week,* November 8, 2018. A discussion of what it's like to live in a state of constant alert, a what-if mentality, and the pervasiveness of mass shootings across our country.

"Understanding survivor's guilt: Parkland, Sandy Hook suicides show lingering trauma." *Today,* March 26, 2019. We have more and more survivors carrying, and succumbing to, the guilt of being grateful for being alive after an incident where others were killed.

"The El Paso Shooting and the Gamification of Terror." *Bellingcat,* August 4, 2019. An inside look at 8chan and the radicalization of young white men who pick up automatic weapons and post manifestos.

"Here's How We Can Prevent the Next School Massacre." *Mother Jones,* April 13, 2022. Adapted from Mark Follman's book on how using what we know could prevent future mass shootings.

"We Have Found One Response to School Shootings: Razing the Schoolhouse." *Esquire,* May 21, 2022. There is a federal grant process to raze and rebuild schools after mass shootings. I find that both horrifying and inevitable.

"I hid from the Texas Tower sniper. His successors have found us all." *Washington Post,* June 3, 2022. Tracing our present back to a landmark event that launched "up in a tower with a rifle" into our vernacular and our cognitive space.

"An American Girl: At 10, Caitlyne Gonzales survived Uvalde's school shooting. Then she became a voice for her slain friends." *Washington Post,* October 24, 2022. This is a searing portrait of a child full of empathy and courage, a survivor of both gun violence and racial profiling. Remember her name.

"The Epidemic of Mass Shootings Is Neither Inevitable Nor Unsolvable." *Mother Jones,* updated May 7, 2023. A Mark Follman essay originally published after the Uvalde shooting, updated after 15 more mass shootings.

"More than 398,000 students have experienced gun violence at school since Columbine." *Washington Post,* as of Sept 11, 2025. The Washington Post project tracking school shootings and the aftermath. www.washingtonpost.com/education/interactive/school-shootings-database/.

"The Key Missing Piece to the Megahit "Adolescence"" *Mother Jones,* September 14, 2025. Mark Follman continues his discussion of research regarding warning signs that identify points of intervention and the "thin line" separating suicidal and homicidal intent in many mass attackers.

"Impact of Gun Violence on Historically Marginalized Communities." *Everytown Research and Policy.* While outside the scope of this book, I should note that the impact of gun violence is not felt equally across all demographic groups in our country. For more discussion and links to research and resources, please see everytownresearch.org/issue/impact-of-gun-violence-on-historically-marginalized-communities/

Poetry Anthologies

Bullets Into Bells: Poets & Citizens Respond to Gun Violence. Beacon Press, 2017. Poems from famous poets followed by commentary from gun violence activists and survivors. The title comes from a poem by Martín Espada, "Heal the Cracks in the Bell of the World," found here: poets.org/poem/heal-cracks-bell-world

American Graveyard: Calls to End Gun Violence Vol 1 and Vol 2. Read or Green Books, 2023 & 2025. Anthology of international poets and authors. The publisher runs a "Sponsor a Senator" program to provide books to legislators and launched a monthly podcast in October 2024.

Further Action

Colorado Ceasefire   coloradoceasefire.org
   Founded in 2000, a grassroots gun violence prevention organization providing education, outreach, and legislative advocacy.

Everytown for Gun Safety   everytown.org
   Formed by a merger of Mayors Against Illegal Guns and Moms Demand Action for Gun Sense in America. Seeks to understand the causes of gun violence and reduce the prevalence.

March for Our Lives   marchforourlives.org/
   A youth-led movement against gun violence founded by survivors of Parkland. Weeks after the shooting, they organized the largest protest against gun violence in history with a march on Washington, D.C., joined by 800 sibling marches in the US and internationally.

Moms Demand Action   momsdemandaction.org/
   Founded by Shannon Watts the day after the Sandy Hook shooting. There are chapters in all 50 states and nearly 10 million supporters.

The Rebels Project   therebelsproject.org
   Mass Shooting and Trauma Support. Founded by Columbine survivors after the Aurora theater shooting, the group aims to connect, embrace, and support survivors of mass tragedy and trauma.

Sandy Hook Promise   sandyhookpromise.org
   Founded by families of the Sandy Hook Elementary School, an organization dedicated to turning trauma into transformation and keeping children safe from gun violence. Maintains the active tipline *Say Something* Anonymous Reporting System, credited with preventing nearly 20 additional school shootings and hundreds of suicides.

About the Author

Elizabeth S. Wolf has published six books of poetry. Elizabeth's previous titles with Kelsay Books are *A Collection of Partings* (2022) and *When Lawyers Wept* (2019). Her *Did You Know?* was a 2018 Rattle Chapbook Prize winner.

Her poetry appears in multiple journals and anthologies and has received several Pushcart nominations. Rattle Summer 2022 featured her project with Prisoner Express. In 2023 Elizabeth taped readings at the White House, Supreme Court, and US Capitol with The Scheherazade Project. Her video poem "April 1999" was screened at the Poetry in Motion Festival 2024 in Colorado. Her work has landed on the moon with the Lunar Codex.

Elizabeth retired from a career in information services and lives in Massachusetts.

www.ingramcontent.com/pod-product-compliance
Lightning Source LLC
Chambersburg PA
CBHW031201160426
43193CB00008B/462